The 12 Disorders of The Toxic Workplace

Finding, Facing, and Fixing the Problems That Are Keeping Your Business From Moving Forward

CARL E. PRUDE JR.

REDWOOD PUBLISHERS

Published by Redwood Publishers
231 East Alessandro Blvd, Ste 111
Riverside, CA. 92508
Printed in USA

Copyright © 2019 by Carl E. Prude, Jr.
All rights reserved.
Rev. 4

No part of this book may be reproduced by any mechanical, photographic, or electronic process, or in the form of a audio recording; nor may it be stored in a retrieval system, transmitted, or otherwise be copied for public or private use—other than for "fair use" (i.e. brief quotations embodied in articles and reviews)—without prior written permission of the publisher.

All accounts, case studies, and stories are true – names of some companies and individuals have been changed for the purposes of confidentiality and privacy.

ISBN 9781711933948

This book is dedicated to all the amazing, hardworking people who brave all kinds of working conditions in order to put food on the table, a roof overhead, smiles on the faces of those you love, and who use your God-given talents to make the world a better place.

Thank you—I hope this book makes your jobs a little easier and a lot more fulfilling.

Also, a special dedication to my wife Imelda, who is the best sounding board, editor, business partner, and friend a person could ever want.

Contents

Chapter 1 – Culture and the Workplace   7

Chapter 2 – Workplace Culture Defined   10

Chapter 3 – 12 Characteristics of a Winning Workplace   13

Chapter 4 – What is a Toxic Workplace   24

Chapter 5 – Workplace Blues   27

Chapter 6 – 12 Disorders of the Toxic Workplace   35

Chapter 7 – Key #1: Stop Asking the Wrong Questions   49

Chapter 8 – Key #2: Don't Focus on the Apple   54

Chapter 9 – Key #3: It's Hard to See the Picture   59

Appendix A: Case Study   65

Appendix B: Case Study   69

Note-taking section for each Chapter - rear of book

Chapter One

Culture and the Workplace

When you step into an elevator and there's only one other person on the elevator, you'd probably politely ask them to push the button for your floor—and then go stand on the wall *opposite* of where they're standing. The last thing you'd do is go stand right *next* to them, right *behind* them....or really, anywhere *near* them!

Why? Because the awkwardness created by merely standing near a stranger in an elevator isn't simply a violation of their personal space, it's also a validation of the inescapable force in society called *culture*.

Whether written or unwritten, understood or not, everything has a culture—even elevators!

In any professional environment, culture, as much as anything else, is the referee for our success or failure, and the scale that measures the value of our education, skillsets, and experience.

This publication addresses one important aspect of culture: culture in the work environment—or *work-culture*. More specifically, it focuses on what is commonly called the *toxic workplace*.

The goal of this writing is to help businesses and professionals gain a better understanding of the inner and outer workings of the toxic workplace. By the time we're finished, we'll have diagramed the most common causes, everyday effects, and debilitating consequences of the toxic workplace. We'll also provide some effective business tools and guidelines to help relieve and resolve workplace toxicity.

Culture is essentially the widely acceptable ways people interact with each other and conduct their affairs—whether the setting be formal, cordial, casual, or professional. Culture is not always logical or practical, but it is functional, unavoidable, and necessary. It helps us accomplish things effectively, and while not always efficient, it helps us organize and manage the chaos around us.

Culture is also a mirror reflecting who we really are and what we really value. It evolves constantly as our priorities and the images we have of ourselves and the world around us changes.

Sometimes this kind of workplace cultural evolution is as effortless and unnoticeable as blinking an eyelash, while at other times it can be as frightening and violent as a high-speed train derailment.

From healthy to toxic, every culture creates and maintains its own eco-system—in other words, every culture has a *feel* to it. That "feel" can be comfortable or awkward, inviting or cold, relaxing or tense, energizing or draining.

But that "feel" isn't just a matter of the general atmosphere of a business, it's an indication of what's important to the business. Instinctively, we often know from the first moment we step into an office if the energy signature is positive or negative. This is usually a reliable gauge for how we'll do if we are hired by that company or have them as a client or business partner.

The cultural environment of any business not only impacts success or failure, but also determines what kind of people can work there. Some work cultures are so good that the people who work in them thrive endlessly. Others are so bad that it's a tremendous challenge for people who work in them to merely survive from one day to the next.

Lastly, there are the highly toxic cultures, which can be so unhealthy, so poisonous, so harmful, that they can be deadly places to work—figuratively and literally.

Chapter Two

WORKPLACE CULTURE DEFINED

Work-culture, work-environment, workplace culture, and work-atmosphere are interchangeable terms that all carry a basic, central meaning captured in simple terms by organizational expert Dr. Samuel Chand:

"This is how we do things here."

For some, this definition may seem too casual—for others, too authoritative. In any case it represents the real margins of a dynamic business environment where the functional and operational boundaries, practices, and guidelines navigate the uncertain arenas of business—just like a football player weaving across the playing field, dodging opposing tacklers on his way to the goal line.

Thinking back to the elevator example mentioned earlier, every business has a unique culture that is built on rules and sustained by guidelines, all which exist to help the business accomplish its core mission of producing and delivering its goods and services.

Some of these rules are written, some are not. Some are formal, some are informal. Some are tried and true, while others are experimental. Some are universal, and some are only provisional, but whatever the case, God help you if you break one of them. You'll be getting an unexpected visit to your cubicle from the culture police—*trust me*.

WHERE DOES "WORK-CULTURE" COME FROM?

The ways in which workplace cultures are formed are as numerous as the different kinds of businesses that exist. The contrasts are as wide as IBM's iconic Brooks-Brothers-suit-and-tie image to the free-styling skateboard-sandals-bring-your-dog-to-work cultures popularized by Silicon Valley tech companies.

Some work culture practices are copied from established business models while others evolve without thought or supervision—forged in the heat of fair competition by the bellows of innovation. Some grow organically, while others come about symbiotically.

Some work cultures are meticulously crafted and orchestrated by an executive team that acts as a master conductor of a symphony, while others teeter on the edges of anarchy, supervised by deadlines, a time clock, and the collective need for a paycheck.

What they all have in common is they exist for the mutual benefit of the business, employees, customers, stockholders, and stakeholders they serve. The actual benefit any of these parties receives is determined, to a large extent, on how and why the specific business culture came to be.

Here's an important fact to remember about work culture: work culture doesn't just appear from thin air; it's intentionally or unintentionally constructed by the constituents of the business environment. As such, it can also be deconstructed or modified to align with the ebb and flow of the demands of business—for better or worse, richer or poorer, in sickness and in health, and in some cases, till death do us part.

Chapter Three

CHARACTERISTICS OF A WINNING WORKPLACE

Before we get into the nuts and bolts of repairing a toxic work culture, let's briefly look at a Winning Workplace to help establish a clearer perspective and set a few place markers that will be useful as we proceed.

Leadership expert John Maxwell says, *"Mechanical systems may be linear but as soon as the human element becomes involved the system becomes both complex and adaptive."*

This points to the challenges that come with bringing people from different backgrounds into a work environment and coming up with practical rules of business that everyone can accept, adopt, and benefit from (believe me, much easier said than done).

No work culture is perfect (because they all involve *imperfect* people), but certain factors must be present (as well as some that must be absent) in order to mitigate the diversity of the human element and the dynamics of the business environment to produce a Winning Workplace.

Here's a list of the twelve most prominent characteristics found in the healthiest work environments, I call them *The 12 Essentials of a Winning Workplace*.

THE 12 ESSENTIALS OF A WINNING WORKPLACE

1) COMPENSATION

In a healthy work environment compensation must be fair and competitive. People who perform at the same levels doing the same jobs should receive the same base compensation, regardless of other distinguishing factors like education, gender, age, or race. Moreover, compensation should be equitable to what other companies within the same industry are paying for similar work.

Compensation doesn't always have to be in the form of a paycheck. Take Todd M., for example. Todd M, a marketing executive with one of the top technology companies in Silicon Valley started out as an unpaid event assistant with an entertainment company.

His initial compensation was only the opportunity to rub elbows with leaders and influencers in the entertainment industry, and he was able to convert one of the relationships he developed into a full-time position with a major Hollywood movie studio, which later became a springboard to his current position as a Marketing Director with one of the top television networks.

2) **CLEAR GOALS**

Most people have heard the famous quote, "Without a vision the people perish". Having a vision of where the company is going is a non-negotiable essential of a healthy work-culture.

A company's goals should not only define where the business is headed but should also provide clear guidelines for how it is determined to get there. In Winning Workplaces the *what* and the *how* are joined at the hip, aligned synergistically with the *why*.

Finally, these goals must be communicated repeatedly in simple terms that are easily grasped, and they must be reinforced regularly both in precept and example.

3) **EMPLOYEE VALUATION**

In the previous section we mentioned the quote, "*Without a vision the people perish*". The inverse of that quote is also true: "<u>*Without people the vision perishes*</u>".

The simple fact is that no business succeeds without the right people. A healthy work-culture places high value on all its employees—from the CEO to the cleaning crew.

That valuation doesn't merely see employees as necessary cogs who make the business work, but also recognizes them as individuals with many other interests outside of work, including health, family, community, hobbies, and faith, just to name a few.

Winning Workplaces do not create unnecessary conflict between the workplace and other important facets of its employee's lives.

4) INTEGRITY

Every Winning Workplace has a code that provides basic guidelines for normal activities and is also used to reconcile conflicts. In many cases, it's a code of honor that's established to help maintain civility and acknowledge humanity within the margins of the formal processes of doing business.

For example, the law-enforcement community has the "Blue Line", the U.S. military has written Codes of Conduct, IBM has their Business Conduct Guidelines, and companies like Coca Cola, Procter & Gamble, and General Electric all have written manuals outlining their Standards of Conduct.

There's even a code of honor among thieves—*at least that's what we're told.*

5) COMMUNICATION

Some of the best laid business plans and innovative ideas die on the broken scaffolds of poor communication. In a healthy business environment, effective communication is never left to chance. Clear guidelines and best practices are studied and implemented so that communication takes place on every level of business in a way that is both timely and clear.

Gossip is discouraged, rumors that could negatively affect employee expectations or damage morale are exterminated with the tools of intentional, timely clear, reliable information. Stratification (aka "cliques") created in the workplace culture by "need to know" and other divisive "communication silo" games are stopped before they can gain traction or momentum.

6) VISIBILITY

There are no bat-caves, secret societies,
or indulgent exclusive groups in a healthy workplace environment—places where only the privileged few can go to hang out, hide out, or otherwise remind other employees that they are not members of the "inner-circle" or "special group".

In a healthy work environment every executive, mid-level manager, and department leader is visible, accessible, and available throughout the organization. Additionally, when formulating business strategies and developing operational best practices, the leadership team values, welcomes, solicits and strongly considers input from members of every part of the company.

7) GROWTH STRATEGIES

A healthy company understands that the one constant in business is not growth, but *change*. It also understands the difference between activity and advancement; recognizing that all movement is not forward, and all change is not progressive. Because of this, businesses with Winning Workplaces™ anticipate, create, and manage growth intentionally.

Comparing your business to a plant, most people determine growth by how tall a plant is, or how much fruit or flora it produces. The same is true for a business—most people tend to measure a company's success by how big it is or how many widgets they sell. However, a lot of important growth takes place beneath the surface as the root system gets deeper and stronger.

Even during frigid winter months when plants appear "dormant", there are still rejuvenate processes taking place that guarantee healthy growth later. Similarly, most growth activities in a healthy business take place beneath the crust, outside the public view.

Healthy businesses implement ongoing strategies that manage important business functions, such as:

- Anticipate and migrate away from expiring products or outdated practices
- Training/equipping workforce to work and think on higher levels
- Strengthen core facets of the business

- Stimulate expansion into new frontiers of opportunity

8) RESPECT

The song "Respect" by soul singer Aretha Franklin is listed by Rolling Stone Magazine as one of the 500 greatest songs of all time. Respect lands at #8 on our list.

An interesting fact about Aretha's signature song is it wasn't originally written or recorded by "The Queen" but by Rock and Roll Hall of Famer Otis Redding.

Redding's version was a lament from a hard-working man who is willing to put up with all kinds of wrongful treatment from his woman—as long as she gives him credit for his hard work ethic and the fact that he is providing for the household.

Respect is the tangible interest that's accrued from the historical contributions of an employee's work, and like interest in the bank, respect carries the same weight and function as any other valuable form of currency.

Respect for an employees' contributions is an essential element in any Winning Workplace—but it doesn't just stop there. In a Winning Workplace, not only is respect given for their contributions, but also for their opinions. Not just for what they do, but also for what they think about what they do.

In a healthy work environment, respect compounds over time, and moves from extendible courtesy to exchangeable currency.

9) **ACHIEVEMENT**

Jonas Salk, the inventor of one of the world's first successful polio vaccines, was once asked how it felt to have made such an important contribution in the field of medicine. His answer was, "I feel the greatest reward for achieving is the opportunity to achieve more."

This points to one of the key elements in every Winning Workplace: achievement. Achievement—whether it be individually or as part of a team effort—is the recharging center for people who participate in a workplace.

With all the ups and downs of business, and all the stresses and challenges of work, achievement is vitally important because it gives people in the work environment a sense of winning, overcoming the odds, and moving one step closer to their goals.

Achievement provides renewed energy, motivation and confirmation that things are going in the right direction.

10) ETHICS

Ethics and morals are two facets of business that are not the same, but because of some similarities they are often confused with each other.

Morality has more to do with what is *good* or *bad* for business, society, and the individual from a *mental, emotional,* and *spiritual* perspective.

Ethics, on the other hand, has more to do with what is *right* or *wrong* for business, society and the individual from a *legal* perspective.

Every Winning Workplace has the commitment to do things ethically and honestly as one of its highest priorities. This commitment is foundational to a business' success. This priority is constantly reinforced throughout the business and demonstrated at every level of business practice.

Having an ethical reputation is one of the most valuable commodities in the business world today—and fortunately, it's not a rare commodity; most business aspire to conduct their affairs ethically. Confidence dwindles and decency fades in the absence of a strong commitment to ethical business practices.

11) PROFITABILITY

If a business is not profitable, it won't be around long. Even large, established non-profits like The United Way or The American Heart Association cannot operate in the red because that's not a sustainable business model.

Every Winning Workplace is either profitable, or in the case of non-profits, operate in the black. Operating in the black is not just a matter of sustainability—it's a sound business practice that many unhealthy companies fail to achieve.

When a business operates in the black it's an indicator that the executive leadership team, department heads, and employees throughout the company are on the same page—operating within a framework that is effective, efficient, and economically sound.

Moreover, profitability provides a layer of security for workers and confidence for banks, investors, financial partners, and stockholders. Security and confidence are two important business attributes that make significant direct and indirect contributions to positive morale in the workplace.

12) LEADERSHIP

If I had to identify the most important factor of a healthy work environment, I would choose leadership. In a healthy work environment, leaders are not just images of people who are smarter than everyone else, or simply who have had successful careers. In a healthy work environment, leaders are owners, participants, mentors, employees, and servants.

Leaders share the credit of a business' success, but they also take ownership of the business' problems and challenges. Leaders in a Winning Workplace take problems personally.

Leaders also participate in the daily activities and operations of business. They don't simply designate or dictate to others—they have skin in the game as well.

Finally, healthy work-culture leaders focus on using their position and influence to make others successful. They're on a constant lookout for other potential leaders who can be developed into future leaders in the business.

Not surprisingly, the companies we've observed with the highest rated Winning Workplaces all have these six leadership essentials in common:

1. Leadership is exemplary
2. Leadership is team-focused
3. Leadership is proactive
4. Leadership is principled
5. Leadership is decisive
6. Leadership is present

Chapter Four
WHAT IS A TOXIC WORKPLACE?

Whatever the opposite of engaging, stimulating, attractive, and satisfying is, that's what a toxic workplace feels like.

A toxic workplace is an unrelenting, unhealthy, repressive work environment that leaves a negative impression with everyone who encounters it. It's like coffee that was once fresh-brewed, aromatic, and zesty, but is since reduced to day-old, gummy sludge stuck to the bottom of the pot, supervised by a hot burner plate that never shuts off. No one in their right mind wants a cup of that.

If we could put a toxic workplace under a microscope, we'd see a teeming collection of sound, traditional business practices mixed with an odd collection of poorly designed systems, unorthodox methodologies, and questionable procedures that all work *together* to work *against* a healthy work environment. From a distance it looks like the classic segment from Sesame Street: "None of these things belong together!"

All toxic workplaces have similarities, but no two toxic workplaces are exactly alike. Each has specific features that creates its unique low-quality index. Different problems in different work settings create different situations for owners, employees, investors, and customers—none of which are good.

But one thing all toxic workplaces have in common is they produce work environments that cost businesses billions of dollars annually. Below you'll find a list of twenty-one detrimental consequences of a toxic workplace; each has a negative effect on business, and each comes with a stiff price tag.

I call this list the *"Toxic Workplace Blackjack Invoice"*, because anyone who doesn't address these issues is gambling with their company's future—the odds are always against you and the bill always comes due!

1. Higher than average turnover
2. Inability to attract or retain top talent
3. High absenteeism
4. Ongoing executive-level attrition
5. Unclear company goals
6. Missed sales objectives
7. Loss of key customers
8. Poor customer service
9. Higher than average occurrence of on the job accidents
10. Low employee morale
11. Few strong relationships among employees
12. Declining productivity
13. Undue mental stress
14. Dysfunctional Teams
15. Infighting between individuals and departments
16. Lack of Creativity

17. Missed forecasts
18. Backwards momentum
19. Little to no innovation
20. High legal costs
21. Absence of fun in the work environment

The most telltale sign of a toxic workplace is simply this: *People don't want to be there.*

Chapter Five
THE WORKPLACE BLUES: REALITY OR FICTION?

n his poem, *Blue Monday*, Langston Hughes writes:

> *Saturday and Sunday's*
> *Fun to sport around.*
> *But no use denying -*
> *Monday'll get you down.*

Scientific research gives us some fascinating data about the phenomenon of "Monday Blues" and the unmistakable link between Monday and the toxic workplace.

According to a CSU human resource study, 70% of all workplace absences take place on Monday. In fact, the number of workplace absences that occur on Mondays are greater than the number of workplace absences of <u>all</u> the other days of the week combined! Additionally, the same study shows the #1 reason for employee absences on Mondays is *illness*.

Another report published on WebMD shows that most heart attacks in America occur on Mondays. The report also showed that most heart attacks that occur on Monday take place before 9:00 a.m.

From all this one thing is clear: the greatest occupational hazard facing today's workplace appears to be *Monday*—especially Monday mornings!

The obvious question is: Why Monday? What does Monday extract from the average worker that the other six days of the week do not? Using the theory of Occam's Razor we quickly come to the answer: the mere prospect of going back to work Monday morning is making people sick.

That sounds a bit frivolous, ironic, and maybe even humorous—but when we dig deeper into the subject, we discover that the real reason people dread going back to work on Monday is not the job itself, but rather *the toxic work culture.*

Winning Workplaces range from *fair* to *outstanding*; conversely, unhealthy workplaces range from *poor* to *toxic*. The unhealthy, toxic workplace is one of the biggest malapropisms in business, on the one hand expecting workers to be upbeat, motivated, helpful, and positive, while, on the other hand, creating an oppressive, difficult work environment that drains them of the very qualities it expects them to demonstrate!

HOW DOES WORK CULTURE BECOME TOXIC?

Sometimes the causes of toxicity in the work environment are obvious—such as a short-tempered manager who blows their top and takes it out publicly on members of their staff. But in many cases, the causes are not as obvious, often hidden within the hems of bureaucracy, tucked away somewhere in the corporate archives, or just stuffed beneath a stack of forms next to the copier.

When working with clients we've seen time after time that just about everyone is aware of the problems created by the toxic workplace culture, but hardly anyone wants to take responsibility for it. That's mostly because they don't know how to fix it.

The prevailing attitude in most businesses is that the task of fixing the broken work culture problems are the responsibility of a yet-to-be-formed department, a yet-to-be-hired person, or a yet-to-be-named team leader.

But like the unwanted pile of poop left on the carpet whenever Aunt Clara visits with her little dog Checkers, there is no scenario in which a toxic workplace cleans up after itself or goes away in time. Like the smelly package from Checkers, the longer toxic workplace issues are left untouched, the more permanent the stain becomes and the tougher it will be to remove later.

Toxic workplace problems are mostly the result of poor decisions, and poor decisions aren't made by computers, logistical processes, or automation: poor decisions are made by people. Almost all toxic workplace problems start out with the one-two combination of these two poor decisions:

Poor Decision #1: Someone introduces something (normally a behavior or an action) into the work culture that offers a provisional benefit to a specific person (or group of people). This action goes directly against at least one of the principles of a Winning Workplace and changes the trajectory of the work environment—even if it's only ever-so-slightly.

Poor Decision #2: Once people realize the first decision is doing more harm than good, it's addressed in one of the two following ways (both of which are ineffective):

A: The first way is to give lip service disapproving the unwanted behavior, but still allow it to continue, even if only in some modified form.

B: The second way is to put an end to the harmful practice but fail to reprimand those involved or put effective safeguards in place to discourage anyone else from trying the same thing. Additionally, in this scenario, after the harmful practice is stopped, the company resumes business as usual as though nothing ever happened.

Here's an example of how easy it is to unknowingly introduce toxicity into the workplace.

Chad worked as a picture editor for a magazine. He'd been there for about a year. Chad normally got off work at 5:00 pm, but because he picked up his daughter from swimming class at 6:30, he usually hung around the office until 6:00 pm.

James, the new operations manager, worked late every night and noticed Chad hanging around the office late every evening. A couple of employees had reported that personal items were missing from their cubicles, and while no one openly said anything, some wondered if Chad might have been involved. Maybe the real reason Chad was staying late was to have an opportunity to steal from other employee's cubicles once they'd left.

One evening, after clocking out, Chad was sitting at his desk drinking coffee when he spilled some coffee on his favorite crimson red "power tie". Chad knew that Sylvia normally kept a Tide quick-stain stick in her top drawer (he had borrowed it on several occasions before), so he walked over to her cubicle, opened her desk drawer, and began rummaging around for the stain stick.

Just as he was reaching into her drawer, James rounded the corner and saw him. "Chad," James said rather cautiously, "what are you doing in someone else's desk?"

Chad explained what happened to his tie, and that he was looking for the stain-stick Sylvia had let him borrow before. "Chad," James said rather uneasily, "we take employee privacy very seriously here, and it looks to me like you're invading another employee's private space without their knowledge or permission".

"Are you accusing me of...stealing?", the words tumbled clumsily out of Chad's mouth like oranges spilling out of the bottom of a grocery bag. "I would never, ever, do anything like that!"

"Chad", James spoke slowly and deliberately, "I'm going to have to ask you to hand over your building pass until we can meet with HR and straighten all this out".

The next day was the day that picture layouts for the magazine had to be approved—normally Chad's busiest day of the month. But when he didn't show up for work with no explanation, it wasn't long before the office whispers started making the rounds.

"Chad was caught red-handed going through several people's desks!"

"The missing items from the other two employee's desks had been found in Chad's briefcase!"

"Chad was getting something out of the trunk of his car and the security guard happened to notice several stolen items inside!"

When Chad came into the office the following Monday to meet with HR, it only took about an hour to clear everything up. However, Chad and James both had to sign NDAs before the meeting, and both were restricted from discussing the matter with other employees.

When Chad walked to his cubicle, he could feel the cold stares of anger on his neck. As he settled in at his desk, he was aware of the side-eye glances of suspicion that his co-workers didn't particularly try to hide. Over the next few weeks the workplace grew increasingly more tense and uncomfortable for both Chad and his co-workers.

The following Monday was the monthly kickoff meeting for the editing team. Chad had thought about skipping the meeting and frantically searched his work log, hoping to find a project to dig into and use as an excuse not to go. The idea of being in a closed-in space with people who were now hostile towards him wasn't exactly something he looked forward to.

In the end, he decided to attend the meeting, making sure to be the last one in. He took a seat in the rear of the conference room, away from the rest of the huddled team. He was surprised to see the head of HR seated in one corner of the conference room with her fingers flying across her laptop keyboard. She had never attended one of these monthly kickoffs, so her presence made him feel slightly uncomfortable.

Shortly the Senior Editor walked into the room, and after a few hellos, asked everyone to get settled into their seats and started speaking, "Before we start our usual planning session this morning, we have some unfortunate business that we need to address. As some of you know there have been some reports of missing personal items from different people's desks."

"We've always tried to build a family atmosphere here, and as such, we take theft very seriously. We wanted to nip this problem in the bud, so a couple of weekends ago we had a security company come in and place cameras throughout the building. Well, it gives me no pleasure to announce that we've found the thief—it was the operations manager we recently hired, James!"

Everyone in the room let out a sigh of relief, and a couple of people glanced around uncomfortably at Chad. Sylvia smiled nervously and patted him on the shoulder as she walked past him.

Nothing else was ever mentioned about the incident from anyone on the senior management level, but unfortunately, a residual element of suspicion and distrust continued to exist in the workplace. This aura of distrust was never addressed directly with the group, and as a result, the work environment never returned to it's previous healthy state.

Chapter Six

12 Disorders of a Toxic Workplace

Although workplace toxicity can be complicated, there are still common symptoms that help us understand where to focus our efforts when looking for causes and answers. In chapter three we introduced the "12 Essentials of a Winning Workplace". We'd now like to introduce their counterparts, the "12 Disorders of a Toxic Workplace".

1) EXPECTATIONS TO PERFORM WORK WITHOUT COMPENSATION

It's unethical to expect employees to work without getting paid. It's illegal to try to force them to do so. As simple and straightforward as this sounds, companies still find plenty of grey areas that give them wiggle room to operate in.

Fuzzy examples of this would be asking an employee to drop a package off at the post office on their way home, or have someone stay an extra twenty minutes after they clock out so they can lock up once the cleaning crew finishes.

A more eyebrow raising instance would be demanding that someone work off the clock to catch up on work that should have been done during normal business hours.

When the expectation to work without pay becomes routine in the work-culture, abuse is inevitable, and the hourly worker is often left holding the short end of the paycheck.

2) **THREATS TO A WORKER'S PHYSICAL WELL BEING**

Typical threats of this nature include threats of physical confrontation, workplace bullying, yelling and other forms of verbal abuse, violating someone's private or personal space, some forms of sexual harassment (which we'll address as a separate issue later), and occupational hazards that pose a threat to one's safety (i.e. a person who is hired as a heavy machine operator but not given proper safety training or safety equipment to prevent injury).

These kinds of working situations occur more often than most of us imagine, in fact, they exist to some degree in every workplace. The only purpose of this type of conduct in the work environment is to influence behavior and exert control over others. These intimidation tactics are usually subtle or implied, but they can easily escalate to the physical level when not treated as a serious threat.

3) THREATS TO EMPLOYMENT BY DURESS

Every job comes with some level of stress. Our normal work responsibilities have some level of pressure linked to the expectations of the job—including the possibility of being fired for nonperformance.

But toxic workplaces take normal job stressors and hurls them recklessly into a mixture of projection and fear to create a foreboding stew of dread and presentiment.

In such an environment, employees are always nervously looking over their shoulders, always dreading unexpected phone calls or emails from superiors, and, in general, always expecting something bad to happen—usually to them.

This crisis-de-jour is usually the by-product of an unhealthy management style intended to create an unsettled work environment—based on the theory that people will be more focused and work harder when they think misfortune is just around the corner.

Hughes Mearns' poem is an illustration of mental exhaustion that wears a person down and pushes them to the brink of paranoia in an environment like this:

Yesterday, upon the stair,
I met a man who wasn't there
He wasn't there again today
Oh, how I wish he' go away....

4) UNSAFE WORKING CONDITIONS

Unsafe working conditions cover a range of occupational hazards that can result in injury to the employee. Some jobs, by nature, are more dangerous than others. For example, sitting at a receptionist desk in a one-story office building presents a much smaller safety risk to the worker than climbing a thirty-foot utility pole to repair a broken electrical line.

Unsafe working conditions factor into a toxic workplace when these work hazards are recognized but proper measures are not taken to mitigate the danger, prevent injury, and insure the employees are safe.

An interesting example was a company in the Midwest that neglected to clear the ice and snow from the forty-five-foot walk path between the covered parking garage and the building. Although many people complained and several employees had slipped and sustained minor injuries, the company still declined to do anything about the problem.

Finally, an employee slipped on the ice and struck their head on the frozen pavement, leaving them in a coma. An aggressive law firm sued the company on behalf of the hospitalized employee, but also convinced enough of the other employees to join a class action lawsuit against the employer.

As a result, the court awarded the plaintiffs a judgement in excess of thirty-million dollars—all of which could have been avoided if they would have bought a few bags of rock salt and paid a high school kid $50 a week to come clean the walkway before going to school each morning.

When employers refuse to take actions to eliminate known safety hazards in the work environment, it results in an underwired sense of apprehension that affects how people work and how long they remain employed. But even more seriously, it could cost lives and millions of dollars in legal troubles.

5) UNETHICAL BUSINESS PRACTICES

Unethical business practices fall into two categories. The first category covers any business practice that's clearly illegal.

An example of this is Otto's Online Auto Parts (true story—fictitious business name), a company that sells discount auto parts over the internet. They have about 65 employees, millions in revenues, and thousands of loyal customers across the globe.

But they also have a big problem. Apparently, most of their car parts come from a network of underground chop-shops run by the co-owners (if you're unfamiliar with the term "chop-shop," it's a facility that receives stolen cars, dismantles them, and sells the individual parts).

This business model was great in terms of producing huge profit margins, but awful in terms of unwittingly involving just about every employee in a federal criminal investigation. That's the type of benefit package nobody wants.

The other category of unethical business practice covers companies who operate on the edge of the law. This includes things that might be illegal in certain circumstances but not others.

A great example of this was a religious non-profit in Texas that provided shelter and jobs for homeless people and undocumented immigrants. Sounds noble. However, upon closer inspection, it was discovered that whatever earnings the people made had to be turned over to the non-profit.

Additionally, the non-profit organization also helped some of these residents qualify for different government assistance programs—the benefits all of which were also turned over to the non-profit.

When the case was brought to court, the non-profit was acquitted because all of the people living in the shelter claimed that they freely donated 100% of their income and welfare benefits to the organization.

In either case, unethical business practices leave a trail of smoke, and where there's smoke there's usually heat, and eventually, somebody gets burned.

6) DISCRIMINATION BASED ON IDENTITY

In the workplace, identity should be a celebration of individuality and uniqueness, but often it's the basis for assumptions that unfairly bundles, marginalizes, and then misrepresents people who, ironically, are often unfairly bundled, marginalized, and misrepresented in society.

Stereotyping is the most blatant example of this kind of toxic behavior, and it can be applied to employees based on gender, race, education, religion, ethnicity, or physical characteristics, just to name a few.

It's difficult to measure the levels of discouragement, frustration, and mental torment that come from working in an environment that factors in your gender, race, ethnicity, etc. when determining your value to the company and deciding what growth paths will be available to you.

Of course, people overcome these challenges all the time, still, this is one of the toughest toxic workplace problems to tackle—because our attitudes towards others are formed over the years and aren't likely to be changed with a human resource meeting or a diversity pamphlet.

7) GOSSIP AND RUMOR

Gossip and rumor are the grease and oil that send the passenger car of trust careening off the rails of progress and crashing into the murky ditch of what could have been. Gossip and rumor are like salt on pork rinds—they help create more of an appetite for something that's not really healthy in the first place.

All toxic workplaces have some trace of this pollutant in the environment, but, when they become a prominent feature in a workplace, the workplace can become inescapably poisonous.

The greatest casualty of this kind of environment is trust. Without trust it's impossible to create or maintain a Winning Workplace. In this kind of environment, the desire to undermined people and processes are valued as much, if not more, than the people or processes themselves.

In his book, The Speed of Trust, Stephen M.R. Covey writes, "while high trust won't necessarily rescue a poor strategy, low trust will almost always derail a good one."

Healthy relationships, strong teams, and sustained progress have no chance of surviving in an environment supervised by a rumor mill.

8) POOR COMMUNICATION

Poor communication occurs regularly in the toxic workplace—expressed mainly in these three forms:
1) *Dishonest Communication*
2) *Unclear Communication*
3) *Poorly Distributed Communication*

1) Dishonest Communication flows from the top down as well as from the bottom up. Managers fudge on their reports and numbers, sales teams create unreliable forecasts out of space dust, and executives say there's no truth to the rumor that the company is relocating, even as the moving vans are backing up to the loading docks.

When unreliable information is regularly presented as factual, it's just a matter of time before the entire house collapses.

2) Unclear Communication can be anything from outright, boldface lying, to the trail of confusion left by poor writing or speaking skills and the tendency to inflate the importance of either the communicator or the message by adding a lot of unnecessary words—word gymnastics that increase misunderstanding rather than clarity.

Additionally, business communication today is plagued with clutter and verbal camouflage. These communication nuisances are responsible for taking simple messages hostage and turning information sharing into ambiguous language crime scenes.

3) Poorly Distributed Communication is the consequence of not having an organized system for sharing accurate information throughout the enterprise in a simple, clear, and timely basis. This kind of communication is the birthplace for frustration, finger-pointing, and a variety of workplace assumption landmines.

These communication problems create a culture of instability, mistrust, resentment, and failure. They're also flagship tenants of the toxic workplace.

9) POLITICAL SHENANIGANS

Most people appreciate a workplace that has straightforward, established guidelines for promotion and reward. The top performers and most effective workers have a clear pathway to career growth based on effort, contribution, productivity, and drive.

In such an environment, employees can predictably and continuously move up the ladder of success (if they so desire), based on clear paths of merit.

However, when those who have rightly earned promotions and bonuses are overlooked in favor of those who have not, it undermines confidence and damages the tone of the workplace—and also gives employees a reason to update their resumes.

The brownnoser, the inexperienced relative, the attractive recent hire, the jerk brought in from another companying carrying a truckload of clients with them, the low-talent person who is always smiling in the boss's face and laughing hysterically at their jokes...these are just some examples of the types of people who cut into the line of logical succession, not based on merit, but based on something else.

Sometimes, the "something else" that explains their promotion might have a viable argument for advancing the business, but in most cases, it results in a person occupying a position that they're unqualified to fill.

Even if there is a strategic short-term benefit to passing up qualified candidates in favor of less-qualified candidates who bring some X-factor with them, when this is a recurring practice in a company, it's always a long-term lose-lose equation.

10) INCOMPETENT LEADERSHIP

When most people think of incompetent leadership, they usually think of leaders who lack the experience, education, or perhaps the resources to be effective.

Those factors are certainly important, but as it relates to the toxic workplace, most cases of incompetent leadership involve leaders who are negligent, leaders who delegate responsibility without delegating authority, leaders who routinely take detours to avoid road hazards in the workplace, and leaders who are absent.

But perhaps the biggest failure in leadership as it relates to a toxic workplace is leaders who are indecisive. By indecisive, we're not talking about people who are merely procrastinating—we're talking about people who have an idea of what to do to fix the problem, but they just refuse to make the decision.

The French use a term, *noblesse oblige* that basically means, those who are placed into positions of leadership must carry out the duties and responsibilities of leadership. The consequences of failing to do so are too many to list here, but with the resources available today, there is simply no excuse for incompetent leadership.

In fact, studies prove again and again that incompetent leadership produces more toxic workplaces than any other factor in business.

11) UNWELCOMED SEXUAL ATTENTION

Whether it's from superior to subordinate, subordinate to superior, or peer to peer, nothing contorts the workplace dynamic like unwanted sexually suggestive behavior (come to think of it, consensual sexually suggestive behavior can also turn the workplace into something of a pretzel).

Some cases are so egregious (like the thousands of terrible "casting couch" stories) that families, careers, and even entire companies have been destroyed by the lewd behavior of workplace paramours and predators.

While it's true that some people find lasting romantic relationships at work, for every office romance story with a happy ending, there are ten thousand stories that end in disaster and complete ruin.

But to be clear, we're not talking about anything romantic, we're talking about inappropriate sexual and sexually suggestive behavior. This kind of behavior is malevolent, adolescent, and draws from the crudest forms of vulgar instinct to act out whatever their twisted imaginations are trying to concoct, somehow unaware that they're probably committing a crime.

Once this type of toxic behavior gains a foothold in an organization, it's usually game over. In almost every situation where unwelcomed sexual attention is a factor, in order to return the workplace to a healthy state, someone has to go, and unfortunately, sometimes it's all the way to prison.

12) BLAME AND GUILT

Blame and guilt are two of the most popular condiments of the toxic workplace. They're used to try to cover for what's lacking in our half-baked business plans and ill-conceived recipes for success. But instead of making the workplace more digestible, they make it more detestable.

In these kinds of work environments, those with power and position often take credit for company successes but push the blame for failures somewhere else. The failure of a flawed marketing campaign or poorly planned product launch is often blamed on some minor task that someone else overlooked or underperformed.

Likewise, the guilt of a department failing to meet their quarterly targets can be placed on some scapegoat who may have only played a minor role in the grand scheme of things.

The two most destructive products of a culture of guilt and blame are stratification and distrust. Employees with titles construct the narrative that allows them to appear to be smart and have business savvy, while pushing the blame for their mistakes away from themselves onto some person or group who they decide are incompetent. Whether that's the reality of the situation or not, it becomes a reality in the work environment where guilt and blame are freely exercised.

Chapter Seven

The First Key: Stop Asking the Wrong Questions

No one said that tackling difficult toxic workplace problems would be simple, quick, or easy. Dealing with toxic work culture issues can sometimes feel like your team is running a sprint relay race through chest-high wet cement.

No matter how arduous or plodding it may seem, the fact remains that work culture problems aren't written in stone, and with the right experience, some proper guidance, strong commitment from the right people, a well-crafted plan, and a heaping scoop of common sense, any toxic workplace can be transformed.

This section presents three of the most important keys that any corporation, business, non-profit, or professional can employ to reverse the effects of a toxic workplace and transform it into a winning workplace that brings out the best in business and in people.

Key #1: Stop Asking the Wrong Questions

At a glance, many work-culture problems appear simple—one or two-dimensional business "speed-bumps" that should be fixable with a few meetings, some whiteboarding, and a little brainstorming. Unfortunately, in most cases the final outcome of such an approach will be about as valuable and authentic as a pair of swap-meet "Addiddas".

Toxic workplace issues are rarely superficial and can run several layers deep. The quickest way to come up with wrong answers when trying to fix them is by asking wrong questions.

Since most work culture-related problems affect our work processes and outcomes, we tend to ask process-related questions when looking for root causes, and outcome-related questions when looking for simple answers to complicated problems.

Here are some examples of the typical wrong questions that fit this category:

1. Do we need to create more balance between work and life?
2. Should we pump in oxygen to help keep our people alert?
3. What technology or software upgrades should we be looking at?
4. Should we get a ping-pong table or pool table for our break room?

5. Employee X seems to be at the heart of the problem...should we transfer employee X to a different department, or just let them go?

Process-centered questions like these assume a solution to a symptom in the work environment, and then seek to prove <u>that</u> assumption—*not discover* the real source of a problem.

We call these process-centered questions, "lotto-ticket" questions. The chances of them helping us find a good, long-term solution to a work-culture problem are about the same as the chances of us buying a winning million-dollar lotto ticket (currently 1 in 302,575,350 for the Mega Million Lotto)!

The only thing lotto-ticket questions are good for is shuffling the same cards in the same deck on the same table. When we go down this dubious path of discovery, all we end up with is a false sense of accomplishment—because, after all, we *are doing something* about the problem...right?

The truth is this strategy doesn't move the needle towards producing the kind of genuine change that businesses and working people need and are really looking for. Lotto ticket questions are like garlic—they should only be used sparingly and very selectively.

Even though the problems we're trying to fix have a negative impact on our processes, most of these work-culture problems aren't process-related at the source—they're usually *people-related*. The root source of most work-culture problems we'll encounter has a name, and that name is usually something like Sam, Janet, Marianne, or Sidney. *Almost every toxic workplace problem we'll encounter is a person (literally caused by a person).*

This isn't to suggest that simply firing, transferring, or replacing a person will solve the work-culture problem your business is facing. That might work in some cases, but people who participate or cooperate with practices that sour the work-environment are usually just taking advantage of situations that exist in the cracks of our corporate guidelines, structures, strategies, or methodologies.

The real key to finding better, long-term solutions is to start by asking better questions.

Better questions look beyond the toxic symptoms, points of failure for a given process, or the general sense of frustration, and mines for 24-carat answers that put our businesses back on track and in alignment with our goals. Better questions uncover the tangled roots beneath the substratum of your business' work environment.

A few samples of better questions are:

1. <u>Who</u> is willing to take ownership of this problem?
2. Does the person who is willing to own this problem have the authority and the resources to change it? (if the answer is "no", it's not really their problem)
3. Who/what are the organizational bodyguards that allow this dysfunctional behavior to continue?

4. Who has the most to lose if this toxic condition _doesn't_ change?
5. Who has the most to lose if this toxic condition _does_ change?

Better questions aren't lotto questions—they're shovel and jackhammer questions. They're archeological in nature—sometimes requiring the bulldozer of clarity or the jeweler's eye of mission—but they always move your business forward.

Chapter Eight

The Second Key: If You Want Better Apples, Focus on the Soil

Today, companies spend tons of money trying to get their target customer's attention. Everywhere we turn we're hit with eye-catching packaging, snappy tag lines, witty jingles, surprising website pop-ups, and slick social media offers—all designed to polish the apple and entice us to take a bite.

If you're in business, you've undoubtedly been tempted to play the follow-the-leader game and copy other popular marketing fads in the never-ending race to be noticed. The buzzword of today's business season is "branding", a term that describes a product or company's reputation as a measure of its currency value or market equity.

Having a clever ad campaign that features a celebrity or an animated rabbit will probably bring attention to your brand, but in most cases this kind of marketing strategy merely allows us to borrow from *someone else's* brand equity and audience to account for deficiencies in our own. The novelty of ad campaigns like this demands they be refreshed constantly to be effective.

But the strongest brands don't rely on outside endorsements or advertising prosthetics to prop them up—

they stand up and stand out on their own. Their branding isn't manufactured by an agency or a marketing campaign—it's organic. So how does that happen?

Here's a clue. Ask any good farmer what it takes to produce crops that consistently bring in more repeat customers than you can handle, and they'll tell you two things. The first is this:

1. If you want better crops, don't focus on the apple, focus on the soil.

The "soil" is the cultural foundations of your business. This covers your values, what you're trying to do, and how you plan on getting it done. It's the visionary and philosophical core of business that determines the overall health, direction, and pace of an organization, as well as the delivery of its products and services.

The nutrients and essential components to support and grow everything you need are found (*or not found*) in the "soil" of your business. Your soil provides a solid base for your business's roots—which will hold your business steady when facing the heat of market demands, the storms of competition, and the winds of change.

The second thing every good farmer will tell you is this:

2. Whatever is in the soil eventually ends up in the tree.

Because of this, it's important to watch for contaminates in the essential growth environment (instead of water, air, and dirt, think people, processes, and products).

Professionals need to develop a keen awareness of incompatible and potentially dangerous elements we introduce to our business environment to make our businesses grow faster or more robustly (for example, we hire a Product Manager who was successful at another company, but whose management style is incompatible with how we want to support our people and deliver our services to the market).

Healthy soil isn't produced by a mission statement or a marketing campaign. What we desire is often expressed in what we say, but what we are committed to is usually expressed in our behavior, which is ultimately and essentially our culture. Consequently, the reality of our business' success or failure will be formed around our internalized commitments, not just our externalized desires.

For example, suppose we have a top sales producer who consistently treats some co-workers and support condescendingly. We don't like their behavior—but we tolerate it because of their outstanding productivity.

We're hoping, with some additional training and mentoring, they'll come around. But in the meantime, every month we continue to overlook their glaring flaws in favor of making a fuss about their sales achievements, including "Salesperson of the Month" plaques, write-ups in the company newsletter, and the corner office with the window view.

I call these high-performing team-disrupting free-radical employees "*NFLs*", which is short for *Not-For-Long*.

The real message being sent (and received loudly) is that we value NFLs over strong, healthy teams.

NFLs can show up in every level of an organization—from the boardroom to the boiler room. Regardless of where you find them, and despite their notable contributions, NFLs will poison your work environment.

NFLs usually have "me-me-me-and-me" tendencies that undermine the principles for building strong organizations and healthy, functioning teams. While their positive contributions to your organization may be significant and desirable, they'll also underwrite poor team performance, workplace tension, and employee attrition.

Besides NFLs, there are many common people and process troublemakers that pop up regularly in today's business environment. The best way to inoculate a business against these harmful work environment contagions is to build up your business' "immune system".

The business immune system is made up of the critical business components that, when healthy, can convert the dirt and scrabble of any business into Miracle-Gro, and produce the types of products, services, workplaces and enthusiastic customer advocates that standout—even in a crowded market.

Here's a brief list of some of these business immune system boosters:

- Practicing Leadership Dynamics vs. Dynamic Leadership
- Creating Prescribed Strategies for Conflict Resolution

- Managing Transition vs. Planning Change
- Developing Organizational Congruence
- Focusing on Employee Development vs. Employee Training
- Avoiding the Good-Looking Me-too Time Thieves that are Vogue on the Outside but Vague on the Inside
- Cultivating Growth Through Employee Engagement Based on Delegation vs. Control
- Prioritizing Clarity over Focus
- Making Principled Decisions vs. Situational Decisions
- Creating an Environment of Diversity without Adversity
- Building Great Communication Pyramids

Chapter Nine

The Third Key: It's Hard to See the Picture When You're in the Frame

Imagine sitting at your desk munching a donut when you suddenly feel an unusual burning sensation in your mouth, followed by your tongue and upper lip swelling up five times their normal size! Question: would you ask your co-workers to form a committee to treat the problem, or would you go see a doctor?

You'd probably go see a doctor—why? Because doctors are specifically and uniquely trained to tell you exactly what's wrong, tell you why it's wrong, and, most importantly, prescribe a treatment to help fix what's wrong. Not only do doctors have the education and training, but they also have access to the tools and specialized equipment needed to fix the problem.

It's just smart to turn to a doctor when we get sick. Yet, when serious work-culture problems develop in our businesses, many companies abandon this common-sense approach of relying on professionals, turning instead to employees who usually have little to no training or track record of dealing with workplace culture problems!

Employees—even executives—are rarely equipped to competently tackle culture-related workplace problems, problems that are usually created, after all, by the way they work! Even though in-house committees are brought together with the best intentions, they usually under-perform in these situations. In fact, studies show that these inhouse teams are 92% more likely to fail than succeed.

Think for a minute—the average employee is hired because they're good at sales, or accounting, or software programming—not solving work-culture health and development ailments. They usually have very limited experience diagnosing work environment problems, and even less experience fixing them.

Yet, this flashing red warning light doesn't keep businesses from revisiting this shallow pool again and again, hoping to fish out solutions to work-culture problems that are often complex, persistent, and can carry serious consequences.

Workplace malignancies like sexual harassment, team dysfunction, intimidation, chronic stress, bullying, lethargy, dirty office politics, dishonesty, or heavy-handedness don't yield easily—and especially not to unskilled hands.

One of the biggest problems with using employees to resolve work-environment issues can be summed up in a statement made by organizational leadership expert, Dr. Samuel Chand, who says, *"Never ask a fish how water tastes—they can't be objective."*

In the same way a high school athlete gets used to the stinky sock smell and musty odor of a sweaty locker-room, employees can get used to a work-environment that reeks with dysfunction and unprofessionalism. To compensate, they either develop a tolerance to the toxic environment, or simply find a practical work-around to the problem.

Whatever the case, the phrase, "this place stinks" loses some of its clout once employees acclimate and become nose-blind to what has rotted in the work environment. It's at this point that your business is most vulnerable to the dangers these problems can expose you to if allowed to settle in your business environment.

These workplace malignancies are often really mountains that have the unassuming appearance of molehills. But, like high blood pressure and other such concealed diseases, they steadily, quietly weaken the essential organic business functions that make productivity and workplace fulfillment possible.

According to Fast Company, the success rate of finding a cure for culture-related problems in the workplace increases by as much as 250% when outside expertise is involved.

THREE TELL-TALE SIGNS THAT YOUR WORK-CULTURE PROBLEM NEEDS PROFESSIONAL ATTENTION

It's true that not all workplace troubles rise to the flashing-red-light level, but how does a company know when their workplace issue can be handled internally versus when they need to consider bringing in a professional?

Here are three warning signs that your work-culture problem needs professional intervention:

1. The problem has forced you to come up with workarounds and work-flow compromises that have now become fixtures in your work environment.

2. The problem is costing your business more than you expected or realize (i.e., increased costs to hire and retrain people to replace the ones who quit, lawsuits from employees and clients, higher absenteeism due to work-related "illnesses" or burnout, higher than normal work related accidents, etc.).

3. The problem has persisted longer than anticipated (i.e., problems that don't go away with time, with firing people, with hiring people, with growth, with shrinkage, with change, etc.).

In shorter terms: the problem takes you further than you thought you'd go, costs more than you thought you'd have to pay, and persists longer than you thought it would stay.

Finding permanent, effective solutions to most work culture problems takes more effort than one or two meetings. It's usually a multi-step process, and here are five essential steps that have play a vital role in every successful workplace transformation:

1. **Identifying** a person of rank with authority who will take ownership of the problem.

2. **Properly** diagnosing the trouble being careful to distinguish between symptoms from sources.

3. **Prescribing** a proven solution that both relieves the pain caused by the symptoms and eliminates the real problem at the root.

4. **Implementing** the solution effectively.

5. **Filling** the void of the unhealthy behavior with healthy practices that promote healthy growth and prevent the problem from returning.

These five steps will help transform any stifling, toxic work environment into an energized, dynamic workplace that people are drawn to and are happy to be part of.

One final consideration is the actual system used to deliver a front-to-back solution. Quite frankly, this is where many solutions fall apart. The best way to do this is to have a solid system. This is how the SCLI defines a great system:

Appendix A

Case Study #1

CREATING FAILURE BY CELEBRATING SUCCESS

Jeremy F is a chemical engineer with a roofing materials company. In order to meet a production deadline for a high-profile customer, Jeremy spent almost 16 hours a day at his office for over five weeks. This put a strain on Jeremy's health and his family life, but at the end of five weeks, thanks to his efforts, the company met the deadline.

As a result, Jeremy was recognized for his efforts which, at the time, were considered well beyond the call of duty. Subsequently he was given a promotion and a raise in salary. Jeremy also received a special plaque and recognition from the CEO at a quarterly "All Hands" meeting.

Other engineers who had worked with Jeremy took note, and soon many of them were spending extra hours at work. The increase in month to month productivity was not just noticeable, it was remarkable! But was it sustainable?

The answer lay in an unnoticeable increase in some other alarming figures among the engineer department. For example, over an extended period there was a slight uptick in absenteeism among the engineers, and an average of 1.5 engineers began leaving the company each quarter for other similar jobs in the same field.

ANALYSIS: The Subtle Impact of a Slight Change In Culture

By rewarding Jeremy for his longer work hours, the company unintentionally sent a message that one of the quickest ways to a promotion and an increase in salary was to work longer hours.

As a result, other engineers began putting in longer hours on a regular basis. The longer work hours were not discouraged by executive management or by department heads, but rather praised. In time, however, the longer work hours began to have a detrimental effect on the engineers' lives at work and outside the workplace.

The detrimental effects resulted in higher incidents of absenteeism because engineers needed to take time off from work for either physical health reasons or to repair damaged family relationships. Consequently, although they liked their jobs, the engineers began to look for similar jobs with other companies where they didn't feel pressured to work longer hours in order to be successful or to earn a promotion.

CONCLUSION & RESOLUTION:

By the time the Executive Leadership Team and the Human Resource Department had identified the cause of the higher rates of absenteeism and attrition among engineers, the harmful pattern of working longer hours was lodged deep within the workplace culture.

The longer work hours that the engineers routinely put in allowed the company to consistently outperform expectations and competitors, but conversely generated off-setting costs associated with the time, effort, and money spent on finding qualified engineers to replace the ones who were leaving.

The leadership team had a general understanding of the problems but didn't really have a clear plan to address them, or a method to correct things without disrupting their momentum and success.

During this time Kevin S., Director of Engineering, attended a workshop on *Building Collaboration Across the Enterprise* and was particularly impressed by a workshop facilitator who taught a session called, "Burn out, Burn up, and Burn down".

It focused on getting the most out of a team through intentional workload balance and emerging collaboration practices. Kevin scheduled an appointment to meet with the facilitator two weeks later to discuss the challenges with their engineering department.

The meeting turned out to be a goldmine. The facilitator was a partner with a business development consulting firm and helped clarify multiple issues related to their problem and give them some options to systematically put the business back on the right track.

Within months they were able to restore balance to the engineering division and simultaneously introduce new strategies that helped them maintain higher productivity results by working together *differently*.

Engineers were discouraged from working longer hours, and company productivity forecasts were adjusted back to pre-Jeremy fiasco standards. These changes produced significant (and in some cases, surprising) results, including the following:

- Attrition among the engineers went from 1.5 per quarter to 1 per year.
- Absenteeism among engineers dropped by 300%.
- Customer satisfaction ratings increased by 8 %.
- Quality Assurance ratings for the engineering team went up by 12%.
- Most unexpectedly, sales margins increased by 6% and profitability increased by 13%.

Appendix B

Case Study #2

THE "VOGUE ON THE OUTSIDE VAGUE ON THE INSIDE" EXECUTIVE

Robert K. was the CEO of a large regional telecommunications company. Glenda O. was his newest hire. Glenda had been a popular business commentator on network television, and her move from television into the business world was well publicized.

When Robert hired her, the publicity from her celebrity status boosted both interest and sales for his company. Robert loved her ability to communicate as well as the energy she brought into a room.

Even though she had no actual experience in telecommunications, and even though she had no actual executive experience in the business world, Robert felt that because of her previous experience rubbing shoulders with leaders in the business community, she had some good ideas, great connections, and would be an excellent choice to lead their new expansion into the desktop video-conferencing market.

The initial staff for this business unit consisted of seven people: three sales executives, two engineers, a project manager and a resource coordinator. These were all experienced professionals—self managed and self-starters—and they went about doing what they could to get the new venture off the ground.

After a few months however it became clear that Glenda was in way over her head. She was more interested in her title as Executive Director of Collaboration and in the optics of her transition than rolling up her sleeves and learning how she could make the new business venture successful.

Her ability to communicate, the energy she brought into the room, and her commanding presence were impressive, but down where the rubber meets the road, her lack of experience and the absence of real-world leadership skills were even more noticeable.

Glenda never quite connected the dots between the theory of running a successful business unit and the reality of putting it into practice. As the flashing yellow warning lights began turning red, instead of raising a hand and getting the help she needed, Glenda just figured she'd keep going with the flow until, hopefully, things would start falling into place.

Well....she did get the "things falling" part right—just not into place.

The new business unit had a few early successes, landing a big contract with an existing high-profile client, and winning several smaller contracts. During monthly company meetings, Glenda habitually took credit for the work that her team was responsible for, but seldom acknowledged their individual roles in making things happen.

This caused resentment that evolved into a wall between Glenda and the rest of the team. During team meetings her staff would listen to her out of professional courtesy, but no one followed up on anything she said—partially because they viewed her ideas as impractical, partially because they had little confidence in her leadership, and mostly because—they didn't like her.

In the meantime, if Robert was aware of any dysfunction in the new business unit, he didn't show it. Instead, he continued to enjoy the media attention Glenda brought to his company.

Because of her addition to the team, his company was featured in Forbes Magazine as well as other prominent business journals. He enjoyed having her accompany his leadership team to business functions and mixers.

The first sign of trouble showed up on a Thursday afternoon when, seemingly out of the blue, the high-profile client cancelled the contract.

Apparently, there had been ongoing problems with implementation and unresolved problems with the original engineering design. The staff had brought these concerns to Glenda's attention on several occasions, but her pride and her lack of understanding how to resolve the problems combined to result in nothing being done about it.

The final shockwave hit the company the following week, when four of the seven people of the new business unit all quit on the same day—three leaving for one of the company's top competitors. Within weeks Glenda also submitted her resignation, having made the decision to return to broadcasting.

This created a lot of negative publicity for the company, which shook the confidence of both investors and customers, resulting in a loss of business, the loss of additional employees who looked for smoother sailing elsewhere, and a drop in the company's stock price.

While having lunch with a business associate, Robert shared his concerns about the problems they were facing. The business associate suggested he call Janet P., a friend who worked for a company that specialized in business leadership strategy, and who'd helped another friend with a similar problem.

Robert called and arranged to meet Janet at a nearby pub after work to discuss his company's situation. During the meeting Janet pointed out that Robert had already dealt with a similar problem many years ago when the business was just growing. In fact, she had used that example as part of a thesis on crisis management.

"Wow", exclaimed Robert in surprise, "I guess I've forgotten more about this business than many people even know". They both had a laugh, but then Janet got very serious.

She sensed Robert had the skillset to steer the company through the rough road ahead, but she also pointed out the importance of restoring the confidence of both employees and stockholders during the process. She explained that her company would serve as a "confidence buffer" and partner with Robert while they developed and implemented a recovery strategy.

Fortunately, everything worked out. As Janet liked to put it, things worked out because the company employees got behind Robert and together, they worked them out as a team!

With his guidance the company was eventually able to stabilize and pull out of the tailspin. There was some painful downsizing, twenty months of financial turmoil, and a lot of tough business decisions along the way, but in the end, they were in a stronger position than when all this started.

FINAL THOUGHTS & WORDS

Thanks for taking the time to read The 12 Disorders of The Toxic Workplace. Our hope is that this material has given you a framework to address the work-culture related issues troubling your business.

This is not a book merely about change. Anyone can change the dynamics of a business by simply bringing in new plants, painting the walls a different color, or getting a new laser printer. But that doesn't improve the underlying problems that plague our workplaces.

This book, rather, is about transformation. Transformation can sometimes come out of change but make no mistake, the two terms are not synonymous.

Change can take place on the surface level, but transformation goes deeper. Transformation in a business often starts when people take workplace culture problems seriously and address them directly with an approach designed for the long game, not just the superficial.

Transformation also takes place when people associated with a business have simply had enough.

When leaders and key people in a business become exhausted with failures, disappointments, and plodding along at a snail's pace, it's at this crossroads they make the serious decision to face and accept both the responsibilities and realities of how workplace toxicity is hindering their progress, hurting their business, affecting their employees, and keeping them from getting to the next level.

Change is often satisfied with the optics of what looks good. Transformation doesn't just stop there, it keeps mining deeper and deeper until it reaches the source and removes the contaminates and pollutants causing the harmful infections of the workplace. Transformation seeks out the processes, practices, and people causing the problems and confronts them with a single-option proposition.

The Work-Life Company is committed to helping you with this critical transformation. Here are three steps you can take today that will help advance the process:

1. Call to schedule a free phone consultation to discuss your particular work culture challenges. The consultation usually lasts between 40-60 minutes, but if you're like most clients, you'll be more than satisfied at the value you'll get out of one simple phone call.

2. If you'd like to receive additional information and tips on topics to help create Winning Workplaces™, click or type this link in your web browser and add your name to the list: www.twlcglobal.com

3. Check our website periodically to see what workshops, seminars, and other events and resources are available.

The good news is that real transformation is within your reach, but it won't happen just because you pick up a book like this, read a white paper, or attend a seminar—that's not how reality works.

Reality doesn't form around our wants, our hopes, or even our desires. Reality forms around our commitments.

If you're really committed to making the changes your business needs, we'd be excited to help. We'd like to offer our resources and expertise to assist and guide your company along the path of transformation.

Our partnership doesn't mean that we'll fix your problems—that's not what we do. However, it does mean that we'll work with you and give you the tools to not only repair dysfunctional workplaces, but also help you create great work environments that can sustain and supply your dreams as your business grows from one level of success to the next.

Remember, the pathway forward always begins with the very next step.

Chapter 1 NOTES

Chapter 2 NOTES

Chapter 3 NOTES

Chapter 4 NOTES

Chapter 5 NOTES

Chapter 6 NOTES

Chapter 7 NOTES

Chapter 8 NOTES

Chapter 9 NOTES

Appendix A NOTES

Appendix B NOTES

ABOUT THE AUTHOR

Carl Prude Jr. is a best-selling author, speaker, lecturer, and the president and founder of The Work-Life Company, an organization dedicated to helping businesses and professionals create Winning Workplaces that bring out the best in business and in people.

Carl spent over twenty years as a business development specialist and technology consultant with companies like Cisco, AT&T, Lucent Technologies, and EIS. He also served as director and Board Member for two non-profit corporations.

Carl's passion is to help working people get the most out of their careers and their lives.

For additional information or other inquiries:

Carl E. Prude Jr.
The Work Life Company
231 E. Alessandro Blvd. Ste 111
Riverside, CA. 92508
www.twlcglobal.com
contact@twlcglobal.com
877-936-6677

www.ingramcontent.com/pod-product-compliance
Lightning Source LLC
Chambersburg PA
CBHW021450210526
45463CB00002B/709